The Shining Path

The Shining Path

W. E. Gordon

ISBN:	Softcover	978-1-5144-6441-0
	eBook	978-1-5144-6440-3

Print information available on the last page.

Rev. date: 12/03/2015

To order additional copies of this book, contact:
Xlibris
800-056-3182
www.Xlibrispublishing.co.uk
Orders@Xlibrispublishing.co.uk
727475

Contents

With love, for Carol, Hannah, Norma,
Bruce, Duncan and Andrew

Preface

One summer's afternoon, after reading some old personal notebooks and journals of mine from the 1960s and 70s, I found myself perplexed and astonished at the course my life had taken. So I decided to write a poem, initially inspired by the opening lines of an early journal entry from 1967:

October flew the coop
and the wind howled for six days

Over a number of months one poem followed another. The result is *The Shining Path:* a poetic narrative winding its autobiographical way across key locations on my life's time-line. But what were these precise locations and what happens when I seek to access them through memory?

According to recent research, our everyday experience of the 'now" consists of a stream of discrete 'present moments' of a typical duration of less than ten seconds. In addition to this, there is the disturbing fact that our **memory** of any past event **is not that event itself**. The experience of re-calling through memory our distant past happens now. Even the telling of something that just happened to us a few moments ago is taking place right now. We also have anticipations of the future, but these too are being experienced now, inspiring and shaping our present state of mind. The same holds true for all visions, dreams and revelations after the fact.

A poem is also and always a dream. It is like a daydream of wish fulfillment. No matter how truthful the poet seeks to be, the content of the poem will always be a work of art, of the imagination, a fantasy - clearly reflecting what the poet in the dream of the poem supremely wishes for. This is why poetic discourse is a type of 'lucid dreaming'. The tight locking of **all our experience** into present moments opens up creative possibilities within those moments. The supercharged at-depth present moment of the poem can become its own place and time. When that happens the poem itself can become a verbal icon or window, through which the light of eternity shines into that moment.

The Shining Path is an intensive exploration of these themes, which requires writing of many things at the same time, not always clearly distinguishing fantasy from reality. In the writing of it, my perplexity slowly subsided as three guiding voices began to emerge from the depths of *The Path*.

- the voice of the poet narrating and reflecting
- the voice of the pilgrim trekking towards eternity's sunrise
- the voice of the warrior of light clarifying and guarding the way

In the concluding notes I aim to be as accurate and comprehensive as possible about any literary 'sources'; as 'everyman', I have not undertaken this journey alone but in the midst of a shining cloud of witnesses.

W.E. Gordon
December 2015

October Flew the Coop

Day Trip
(as remembered)

October flew the coop
and the wind howled for six days

white sun dust in my eyes
dust on my books and
between the sheets of my bed
during the day
I leave the back door wide open
to let the sunlight in

at the back of the
white-washed house
is an area protected from the wind
a clump of stunted trees
the size of bushes
and an old stone wall

there the early morning sun
pours down slanted at an angle
onto the parched ground and
into the sides of crumbling walls
dissecting the brown fields beyond
space is luxurious and timeless here
like in American deserts

two days ago storm waves
pounded over the cement
benches in high plumes of
spray six feet high

on my day trip
from Formentera to Ibiza
the little boat Joven Dolores
tossed about so much
I had to lie down flat
holding on to both sides
of the green plastic bench

I had a sense of impending doom
not urgent catastrophe
but something more profound
something more important
something wider deeper higher wilder
that I should be reflecting on
something that was still unknown to me
starting to gently touch my heart
something no one had ever taught me
(at least in language I could understand)
something I had never experienced before
something illusive yet crucial
both weighty and lighthearted
something pregnant with destiny
always escaping me vanishing
before my eyes everywhere I looked

yet something is impelling me on
as it keeps drawing me in
I can only hope that I will find it
on this reckless but determined path I'm on

at the horizon the sunrise
is still angry and red
with bloody streaks along
dark fast-moving elongated clouds

white sunlight suddenly
bursts forth all about me

slicing the mast in two
Ibiza is lying before me
shining brightly in the sun

I am now sitting in Bar Botega Victoria
drinking a cup of coffee
in the old section of the town of Ibiza
just a few yards from the entrance to the old city
a dirt and cobblestone street runs past the door

the wall encircling the city is Roman
high thick cracked archways and stone chambers
the old city is a maze of steep narrow streets
with white-washed house balconies

each with a little yellow canary in a cage hanging
in the open window with the cage door wide open

the canaries fly about free in the crisp
November air roosting and happily chirping
on the black iron railings and under the eaves
the air is still cold
though the sun is slowly warming it

the hills behind the town protect it
from the wind which is now no doubt
full of dry leaves mist and ocean spray
moaning over the flat bed rock of Formentera

The Notebook

This day is significant for me
because I have bought this notebook
with numbered lined pages to write in

my passion is to become a scribe
not just of words and deeds
but of the invisible and the infinite

so here I am sitting with pen in hand
at a table in the grand Bar Botega Victoria
with a warm cup of coffee in my hand

at the top of page one I write

"O selfhood estranged and wandering!
You and the cold pride of life!
a single star reflected in a pool
left by the rains of night!"

❧

I grew up absurd in America
during the 50s and 60s
under blue suburban skies
I was born restless
intimidating and enquiring

I provoked consternation
everywhere I went
I deeply irritated my teachers
and made trouble at school

as I grew up I was indoctrinated
into the half-light and half-truths
of Cold War propaganda

I heard the clarion call echoing
from the depths of Zarathustra's cave
proclaiming the death of God
the end of history and the last man
standing at the end of time
dressed in a grey flannel suit

I was preoccupied with apocalyptic
visions of The Bomb
enormous mushroom clouds boiling and towering
over New York London Moscow and Rome

at University I caved in
utterly defeated
to confess with all the rest
inflexible commitment
to the uniformity
of natural causes
in a closed system
where everything
is reduced to the
contingencies of time
plus chance plus nothing

I read Beyond Freedom and Dignity
The Origin of Species
Das Capital
The Interpretation of Dreams
The Will to Power
Being and Nothingness
Being and Time

and many other revolutionary texts
that put my whole life into question
and my thinking to the test

I put on a white coat and
spent hour after hour
in the psychology lab
experimenting with rats
through controlled experimentations
it became increasingly clear
that for mice and men
operant conditioning explained it all
behavioural psychology
linked with neuro-science
explained away
the meaning of life and
through reason yoked
with empirical science decisively
exposed as pure delusions God
self consciousness and free will

Dawn Apocalypse

I have seen the rise and fall
of global dream-worlds
I have seen the passing
of mass utopias East and West

but mine is the
generation of
total liberation

we advanced together
like an army across the land
hearts hardened and sharpened
into intellectual spears
(there were no tears)
we shot ahead of us volleys of
long-winged arrows of flaming thoughts
into the darkness of the night

we opened wide the doors of our minds
through sexual and political liberation
through the liberating power
of psychoactive drugs
through the liberating power
of the hedonistic calculus
and through the liberating powers
of bebop jazz and rock and roll

we cleansed our minds
and renewed our hearts
in the liberating powers
of anti-colonialism
in the liberating powers

of anti-capitalism
in the liberating powers
of anti-communism
through the liberation
of the forces of production
through the liberation
of the forces of destruction
through the liberation
of unconscious drives
through the liberation
of our naked bodies
through the liberation
of our naked souls
and through the liberation
of all the arts through
releasing the powers
of criticism and anti-criticism
with new visions of
representation and
anti-representation

but we were at our best
immersed within the intoxicating
painted word and abstract expressionism
in hot pursuit of the wayward
transgressing transformative and
radically incomprehensible sign

we experienced freedom of
interpretation through baptisms
into the hermeneutics of suspicion
and we were all given new identities
and alternative versions of who we were
what we were who we had been
and where we all were going

But now that the orgy is over
now that the chips are down
now that the Western sun is setting
casting shadows across the ground
the Owl of Minerva takes flight
she spreads her wings only with the falling
of the dusk at the edge of night

it's only after the defining moments
of our age have come and gone
that discernment begins to come
with the sap of the next age rising
not without pain within the vine

we lived wildly and intensely in our time
at the centre of the storm that had come
and were unmindful of what was said and done

At this point secular philosophy
protesting must give way to prophesy
which compels me to say -

"Do not be deceived God is not mocked
because what goes around comes around
and what we sow is what we reap"

at dawn I lift my eyes to the horizon
as far as my eyes can see
and I see gathered there
massive storm clouds rising
with great shafts of lightning
striking the shores of the sea

and I see signs above
and wonders below

with the sun turned to darkness
and the moon turned to blood
for the great and terrible
day of the Lord has come

The Ancient Starry Dynamo

I meditated on
these gloomy thoughts
for many months until
one winter's solstice
in the kitchen
washing dishes
listening to the radio
I experienced the
opening of eternity in time
within the lyrics of a popular song

when all the dishes were done
I walked out the door into
the freezing moonless night
to see scattered across
a cloudless sky
millions of stars
sparkling like diamonds tossed
across a black velvet carpet
by one sure sweep of a giant's hand

I looked more closely
and saw that these stars
were compacted together
caught in the iron grip
of some nameless power
greater than themselves
around and around they circled
in slow motion held within
gigantic timespans connected
in geometric patterns
large or small
motionless in time as they

took part in some
wild dervish dance
within the wide spiralling
arms of the Milky Way!

O how I would love to join in that cosmic dance!
O how I would love to be fully embraced
within those lovely milky arms
and to be deeply moved within myself
by the love which moves the sun and distant stars!

If I throw caution to the winds
who knows what might begin?

Who knows what might happen
to anyone who dares to dream with God!

We will inspire new prophecies
We will inspire new revelations
We will passionately promote
regime change everywhere

My homeless mind was burning hot
for that heavenly connection to
the ancient starry dynamo
in the machinery of night
but had no connection
to that ancient power
only grim determination
to break out of the Asylum
I was in with no clear path to follow
and no compass to indicate
where to go with whom or to what end

so I hit the road again

trekking towards distant shores
researching ancient books
deciphering arcane texts
digging up old roots
drinking from holy wells
seeking that Ariadne thread
that would lead me
out of the labyrinth I was in

A friend of mine once
said after years of trying to
braid ropes of sand

"What first convinced me
was not necessarily true
it was merely convincing
to me at the time"

then he said
with some remaining grains of sand
still flowing through his hands

"What now seems true to me
by good and necessary consequence
may not necessarily be true at all"

he said this with great conviction
while washing his hands over and over again
he then dried his hands furiously
on a paper towel turned his back on me
and walked out the door

"The whole problem
and the nature of the problem itself
must be redefined"

another friend of mine once said

"There are only radical solutions left
no half measures will do

this is because things are very bad
far worse than we had at first supposed
and things are getting worse
and we are in the middle of it all"

Lucid Dreaming: A Story in Four Parts

Taking Leave

Less than halfway through
my tempestuous life I awoke
to find myself far off the beaten track
blinded by flashbacks
bullied by strangers
my ultimate destiny eclipsed

I was all alone
The straightforward path
I could no longer find
or call my own

turning first to the right
then to the left I quickly
lost my bearings and
wandered into a
forest so strange and dark
I found myself inside
the weirdness and wildness
of my own heart

this momentous event
defined both my state of mind
and the strange place I was in

both inscape and landscape
were in full agreement
each reflecting
the other from the start

There are no maps for
places or times such as this
there can be no
exact ratio of word to thing
although I heard rumours
of a shining path running
through it all
known only to the few

it takes many turns of the screw
to keep our worldviews intact
to keep up appearances
while ignoring the
ever deepening rift
opening up between
appearance and reality

our mind-forged manacles do their job
tightening around our wrists until
the red blood begins to spurt and flow

exhausted
I lay down to sleep
in the deep long grasses
by a tree

I looked up through
the leafy branches to
the starry constellations

I could feel the whole planet
moving slowly underneath me
a whole world turning
from dusk to dawn

At a Liberal Arts College
I was once challenged
by the academic powers that be
to demonstrate just one sign of divinity

within myself or in the world
or at least some innate moral law
corresponding to what I saw

but on their terms I totally failed
I could find nothing at all
not even ancient signs
scratched on a wall

even the memory of
such signs or places
had been mysteriously
effaced and white-washed over

or intellectually suppressed
or reduced to
material presuppositions
and historical perspectives

I could only reply by saying

"If the need to let suffering speak
is a condition of all truth
why are so few speaking?

Why does no one speak the truth
of what must be said?

In the place of truth
all I see are
counterfeit doubles of God
authoritatively proclaiming
a one dimensional man
inside a maximum security
birth-death universe
with CCTV cameras everywhere
hidden on every street"

I balked at this reduction
I refused to accept this conclusion
I kicked back against it
pulling violently this way and that
like the stubborn horse or mule
needing bit and bridle
to keep it to the path

so despite the pain and fear
I strengthened my resolve
threw all caution to the winds
and kicked over the traces

Descent into the Realm of the Dead

I was then unexpectedly
overwhelmed by a vision
so severe so bleak so depressing
I'd rather be dead or snuffed
out of existence altogether
than be trapped alive inside it!

I saw all about me
a howling wilderness
purged of green
purged of colour
purged of sound
purged of song
purged of alphabet and number
so that no word could be spoken
no symbol expressed
no figure drawn to represent
that forsaken place
where all voices are spent

in this vision I saw my own
mind in eternal conscious torment
I saw entire nations and kingdoms
engulfed in flames of wrath
ignited in white-hot interdiction

I saw the wisdom of the ages
burnt to white ash
blown upward
and away by the wind

I saw all human history
(and its memory)
going up in flames

I saw the whole planet burnt up
in flames of lust flames of greed
flames of hatred flames of money
flames of industry
and flames of war

beneath those burning sands
in the darkest regions
of the human mind
I could see whole worlds
lost beyond recall
entire populations and nations
lying prostrate
moribund unconscious
on a shoreless sea
of dreamless sleep

every soul lay floating senseless
forgetful of what was or could have been
each prisoner held in a gigantic web
spun from the chthonic depths
raging and turning in the roots of time

Could this be the place and time
for our reawakening?

Could this be the time and place
for the spirit's coming
and for the universal restoration?

spirit hovering over the
furious primeval seas
sowing into wild chaos
seeds of eternal light

Sleepers awake!

open wide your eyes!
arouse yourself from death to life
and see who brings you light!

with clarity of mind

look within yourself
see with eyes wide open
the visions that come by day
be amazed while fully conscious
at the lucid dreams
that come by night!

The Village Clocktower

One warm summer's evening long ago
I lay tossing and turning on my bed and
as I slept I dreamed and in my dream
and saw a gigantic wheel touching
both heaven and earth
revolving slowly within itself
with smaller wheels spinning
faster and faster inside bigger wheels

echoing in the midsummer's air
I could hear the melodious bells
of the village clocktower
chiming out the hours

between the bells
between two and three am to be precise
I felt someone whisper in my ear
as a spirit drifted past my face

moonlight flowed through
the open bedroom window
filling the room with light

a figure
at first indistinct took shape
like a silhouette carved out of light
and something like
a book was in his hand

the figure then spoke to me and said:

"I am the angel Raziel
The angel that safeguards
the mysteries of the Most High
this book is for you

I have been sent to guide you
and to make you wise
through the contents of this
book I have in hand

reading it will awaken you
and change you and open you up
to truths you have never known before

this Book of Life will
comfort and guide you by
daily reading on the way"

"But how can I know that this is true or real?"

I asked

with that
and with no warning
he grabbed me by the ear
and firmly pulled me out of time
and took me on a whirlwind tour
of 7 heavens and as many hells
right up to the Throne of God
where we had deep conversations
and I heard things unutterable
which I still cannot remember

Raziel Points to the Shining Path

I returned days later beside myself
and sat for hours astonished
and dumbfounded on the floor
with my back against the door

the doors of my perception
were still wide open
I could not close them
my mind was still expanding
beyond all knowing
at what I'd seen and heard

"Forget all that" said Raziel

"The Way to Life
cannot be found
up here above the clouds

but only down there
upon the ground
through new birth
and forgiveness of your sins
on the path that shines
the path that runs through
this world to the next incarnate
in the Word made flesh

but to enter this path
you must first
take revolutionary action by

turning from darkness to the light
opening your heart wide and keeping it open
to the burning flames of love and grace

you must turn around within yourself
and walk on the path revealed therein"

love was burning with
increasing zeal and joy
all about me and within me
as I seized that day

wholeheartedly
cutting off every proud
and haughty thought
that blocked or obscured
my path leading
to the King of Light

through the
power of the spirit
I boldly entered
taking up each day
the sword of the spirit
to cleave the
darkness from the light

I then asked Raziel
who was about to leave

"What was that wilderness and
what that hellish world
unfolding in these visions
I have just passed through?"

his mild and friendly face
became severe and fierce
his whole body began to tremble as
he turned incandescent and unfurled
his enormous golden wings

"That place"

he said

"That place is called the Valley of Decision
multitudes multitudes in the Valley of Decision"

Song of the Dead Leaves

Song of the Dead Leaves

Dead brittle autumn leaves
red yellow orange and brown
no longer pressed
within old note books
because I have opened
all the books and
myself become
an open book
with past present and future
stretching out before me

fallen leaves
of memory stirred
by fresh breezes
gently swirl over cobblestones
around my feet where I stand
(now in memory)
amongst autumn's leaves
heaped up in small piles
up to my knees
against the broken walls
not as they are now
but as they were then
1967
remembered
48 years later through
poemscapes pressed
between pages of
old notebooks and journals

the typewriter print has
faded so much that

some of these pages
yellowed with age
can't be read without
minute inspection

ꙮ

What is this fresh breeze I feel
stirring gently within me?
bringing new life
to what was dead or dying
could this be the breath of the almighty
moving in me and all around me
in visionary perspective?

the moon was much larger then
whiter more intense than now
riding above the gathered clouds
high above the laughing mountains
a solitary witness to the wreckage
and twisted debris in the mudflats
of the flooded plain below

the evening before the
wild storm struck
I saw a black crow
flying just after sunset
in the half-light
between the great palm trees
of the city gardens

several weeks later
the moon eclipsed
to became
a window of obsidian
newborn and polished

today I once again see
the sun relentlessly
pursuing its daily round
descending into darkness
then rising up newborn
exploding the eastern horizon
in primordial elemental fire
as it always has done
since the remotest past
when the planets formed

nothing escapes its rays
no one dares to look
directly at the sight
where every eye is blinded
with excess of light

what kind of music still remains?

what songs are still to be sung
above the twisted ruins of this flood
above these mountains
beyond that flooded plain?

what music still echoes
inside these old books
these journals of mine?

where precisely are those
swirling leaves now gone
along with that black crow
still on the wing
(those many years ago)
flying in bright moonlight
through the palms?

where now is the
morning and evening star?

Where now are the grand
themes of love and war
amongst the billion billion galaxies
expanding now and forevermore?

Time and Eternity

The Song

I wrote a poem today
whether in the past
or present I cannot say

my past is still alive within me
the full meaning of both
the present and the future
remains partially hidden in my past
requiring a poetic theory
of excavation and exploration

no matter what people may say
when I undertake a task like this
many interpretations come into play

as I write these lines
I split off from normal ways
of seeing hearing thinking and feeling
I lose my bearings
I am de-centred raptured
upwards and outwards
my awareness expanding
in the immensity and
boundlessness of it all
I am then cast down dejected

but not for long

I am soon lifted up again
somersaulting as if in play
within the updrafts of the spirit
a whirling gyre of bright wings

my mind is sharply focused
my tongue is set on fire
my heart is held captive to its song
echoing everywhere all day long

The Man from Heaven

Prophetic speech
begins in the depth of night
under degradation
oppression and despair
where the truth is
totally eclipsed

because revelation begins at night
many will never see it or hear it
because of drunkenness or sleep
or hardness of heart or disbelief

but when the spirit comes God-breathed
like the wind blowing through the trees
take a deep long breath within it

if you dare

the sun will then shine for the
children of wisdom at midnight

I am baptised every night
into sleep (that little death)
where my soul is caught in
an opaque whirlpool of
enormous recurrent dreams
not remembered seldom told

as I lie awake in summer
listening through my open window

to birds singing at the break of dawn
I too am brought with joy
to the beginning of the day

as the wind passes through
the strings of an Aeolian harp
I am touched with the songs of birds
with new insights

into the oracles of God
and the
interpretation of dreams

I was roused from sleep
on a mountain top
in Switzerland aged 24
I had fallen asleep
some 10 years before
as a foot soldier
marching headstrong
in the armies of the night

I was a pilgrim on a quest
for the holy grail
lost in the labyrinth
of this world

while pondering
such things a bright
light burst upon me

raising my eyes towards it
I saw the upper window
of my soul filled with brilliance
out of which a man came down

this Man from Heaven said to me:

"Welcome welcome
my dear son and brother
Where have you been my son?
Where have you tarried so long?
Where have you travelled?
What have you been seeking in the world?"

The Cliffs of Inis Mor

I know at first hand
the noise the storm and stress
the restless discontent
of petulant youth

I know the wisdom of sitting quietly
doing nothing in the gentle sunshine
with autumn's golden fruit hanging
heavy on the vine

as I know myself *utterly unique*
so I know myself *as everyman*

standing on the
Irish coast in Galway Bay
watching the Atlantic waves
breaking with a roar violently
again and again against
the limestone cliffs of Inis Mor

each wave is raised up
in plumes of spray
like white sea horses mounting
the dark green walls

only to fall back again crashing down
to the plaintive cries of seagulls
circling high above the mighty roar

here also time and eternity meet
each reflecting a mirror image of the other
two sides of an ancient coin
eternity and time collated
bound together in one vision
which is also a story
knocking at my door

this story has fallen
upon my tongue to tell
tuning it and turning me around
inside myself I reach outside myself
to catch the words
in flight rising to my lips

Poems

Poems first rise up silently
by stealth invisibly
ascending upwards from
from unconsciousness
to consciousness then
scribbled down in haste
on scraps of paper
lying around the house
or perhaps
in some random notebook
lying open on a table
or typed up with care
on a computer screen

but poems rise up
full-blooded only when
they break free
and fly off the page
into the surrounding
air we breathe
with the
poet's voice strong and clear
intoning acoustic
waves vibrating
in our ears

Rhymed Words

Poems and rhymed words
are strong feelings giving
shape and meaning to sounds
that stir the blood
as we dance around
to tunes melodious
or discordant
rhymes and rhythm
recited fast staccato
intoned slow and low
long or short
each syllable crystal clear

opening up new
pathways to my heart
revealing me to myself
at peace or at war
with the universe
bearing witness to itself
in seen and unseen realms
telling stories new and old
by naked words alone
I transmute lead to gold

The Ancient Bard I Sing

The Ancient Bard
I sing:

when I see in
the opening morn'
an image of
truth new born
I can hear the voice
of the ancient bard

the bard is ablaze with light
speaking in tongues
prophesying and singing songs
while standing on a
mountain top at dawn
mountain peaks rise up
sky-clad all around him but
he soon disappears from sight

bright clouds tinged with gold
now swirl around the place
where he once stood and
I can hear the morning star
singing to herself as
she too fades from sight
in the dawning of the light

Amongst other Types of Poets

Amongst various other types of poets
are philosophers thinking serenely
in transcendent realms of light

while the dawning of
eternity's sunrise
incites on the street
revolutionary action
intoxicating speech

poets are also bebop jazz scat
artists or hiphop rappers
seeking 12 Step awakenings
in tower blocks and flats

middle-class middle-aged poets
wander aimlessly in a maze
tortured by their destiny malaise

I now turn the clock back 60 years
to see thin and wasted 1950s
New York-San Fransisco poets
beatific angel headed hipsters
on the nod over the body of bliss

Desolations of Moloch

The universal presence of evil
and suffering in the world
out of sight not out of mind
catches me unaware sometimes
shocks me momentarily
tying me up into knots so I trip
and fall over myself down
amongst the bones of the dead
lying in some vast killing field
that stretches out to the horizon
as far as my eyes can see

while lying there paralyzed
amongst the sun-bleached bones
I see our cities and towns growing
ever harder, crueler, darker

a terrible vision of evil
passes before my eyes

I see Moloch:
that traitorous Watcher
once an exalted son of God
turned a corrupted Elohim

expelled from heaven's gates
thrown down into the
darkness of a raging void

Moloch is
Cast down out of heaven
thrown out of the
heavenly council
denied the bliss of heaven

he falls to earth like
a blazing meteor arcing
across the sky at night
a fallen star from heaven

he hits the ground hard
exploding pent up rage
his fierce demonic speeches
echoing across our planet extol
hatred of God the earth and mankind
inspiring the spirit of our age
breeding monsters of the mind
and giants in the land

The Hammer and the Anvil

In the hands of
a Warrior of Light
our earthbound stories
become a sword of lightning
unsheathed
consuming
the scabbard
that would conceal it
signalling a victory of light
over chaos and old night

as sparks fly upward
when the hammer
strikes the anvil
I am hard at work
at home with sweaty
arms and torso glistening
in the dark smithy of my soul

all about me I see
a majestic opening
of the structures of time

My imagination is released!
My tongue at last can speak!

I am now free and bold
enough to unfurl the total
contents of my mind
into the universal light
of the age to come

when I see that
feelings are just
the visible face of
invisible thinking

I relax effortlessly
into clarity of vision
which compels me
to prophesy over
the ancient ruins and
desolations of time

so I pray for all:

oceans
    mountains
        valleys
            rivers
                forests
                    trees
                        hill-tops
                            grasses
                                flowers
                                    men and women
                                        cities and nations

at daybreak

I rise to consciousness
my mind opening
to the light of day

I see God's glory in
salvation through judgement
I see through the present
into a world to come

I see universal restoration
I see all things washed
and transfigured in the
blood of the lamb

I hear ancient fallen
creation singing
the song of its redemption
as it is lifted up
out of its ruins
victorious in joy
unimaginably full of glory

Seeds of Life

(1)

Within each new-born
babe's primal scream
is planted with infinite
love and care
one indestructible
eternal spark or
seed of light
enclosed within itself
held tight
within the perimeters
of the cyclic powers
of death and life

but if this seed
with its hard heart
is to play its part
entering a
deeper higher life
it must first by death
be slain and torn apart

the heavenly spark
must fall into the darkness
of the ground
and die

in its own season
for its own reasons
it will rise again
to the light
as a tree with branches

growing from that seed
with healing in its leaves

(2)

Death or some
reasonable facsimile
of death is thus
required to make a
sharp distinction
between life and death
light and darkness
spirit and flesh
soul and body
ego and self
kernel nut
wheat and chaff

the imprisoned seed
(or spark)
is set free by
cracking open
the external shell
of the hard dead self
through at depth
ego-deflations
and spiritual
awakenings
within the
Tree of Life

(3)

So let us celebrate
together that
Great Day
by lifting up to heaven

all those lost and wandering
sparks from heaven

let us love them
and care for them
by shepherding them
back into the
infinitely
incomprehensible
omnipresent
Fires of Love

(4)

And so it is that
every letter vowel
and syllable of a
new-born song
will taste to us
first sweet
then sour or bitter

because a fiery spark
of life is embedded
in every word of it
and all the powers
of heaven and earth
interact with it
while each power
mirrors all the others
in joyful self-abandonment

Selah

As these last words are written
I sit down serenely unattached
all conflicts ceased

wordlessly I sit in the
presence of the Prince of Peace

but within these meditations
I am engulfed in flames -
I am burnt up silently -
yet I remain unburnt -
like Moses' burning bush

I am a self-consuming artifact
opening up inside
the New Jerusalem
a metaphysics of Light.

&

O my love
how I do kiss
and cherish
your stones!
your
jasper - sapphire
emerald - gold
sardonyx
topaz - amethyst
lapis lazuli
glass and pearls

the dust upon
your bare feet is
even now
sweeter than honey
to my taste

❋❋❋

O pale scholar!

LOOK UP

Be transfixed in wonder!

A Pure Land
in a Pure Sky

Be ravished!

Rend your books
as your heart is
rent asunder!

Notes for the Shining Path

I am aware that 'Shining Path' is also the name of a Peruvian Marxist terrorist group, with whom I have no connection. I here appeal to and exercise poetic licence, and reclaim the metaphor to give it a different meaning.

The notes below give details on sources alluded to in each section.

Preface (ix)

"a typical duration of between 2-8 seconds."

Stern, D. N. (2004). *The present moment in psychotherapy and everyday life*. London: Norton & Company. (p.23, 26).

"the poem is also and always a dream"

W.C. Williams sees the subject matter of the poem as its 'materials', and borrows from Freud to call the poem, like a dream, 'a space for wish fulfillment'. The subject matter (or materials) of the poem is seen as a fantasy, while the reality of the poem is its structure and 'measure'. Williams sought (along with other modern early 20th century poets like E.E. Cummings, Marion Moore, Charles Olson and Robert Creeley) an innovative approach to structure and measure (metre and rhyme). Citing the 'rigidity of the traditional poetic foot, as a significant obstacle to contemporary poetry', Williams complained that 'our poems are not subtle enough, the structure and staid manner of the poem cannot let our feelings through'. Williams, W.C. (1948) *The Poem As a Field of Action.* Available at:
<http://www.poetryfoundation.org/learning/essay/237854>

I have sought in *The Shining Path* to return to this modern and post modern) view of the poem where rhymes are emergent (not set to the metronome type rhyming) and the metre and line-length is variable expressing or seeking to capture the energy of thought and feeling while sometimes exploiting the ambiguity created by lack of punctuation and blending together past and present moments in time etc.

Preface (x)

"invites the imagination to refine, clarify and intensify those moments"

William says: "To refine, to clarify, to intensify that eternal [present] moment in which we alone live there is but a single force - the imagination."

Williams, C.W. (2015). *Spring and all.* Martino Publishing: Contact Publishing. (p.3).

p.7

re. Zarathustra's cave and the death of God

The philosopher Fredrick Nietzsche originally announced the modern 'death of God' in his philosophic prose poem *Thus Spoke Zarathustra* (1891)

Kaufmann, W. (1970). *The portable Nietzsche.* Viking Press. (p.124).

"the end of history and the last man"

Fukuyama says: "The end of history will be a very sad time."

Fukuyama, F. (1992). *The end of history and last man.* London: Hamish Hamilton.

"the man in the grey flannel suit"

Wilson, S. (1955/2005). *The man in the grey flannel suit.* Penguin Books.

Both a 1950's novel, and a film of that name, was about the American search for meaning and purpose in a world dominated by big business and 'the military industrial complex'.

<https://en.wikipedia.org/wiki/Military–industrial_complex>

re. the Atomic Bomb

I read a lot of 'beat' poetry during this period my life, notably Alan Ginsberg, Jack Kerouac, Gregory Corso and others, but especially Gregory Corso's chilling *BOMB*.
Corso, G. (1958). *BOMB*. City Light Books.

"uniformity of natural causes in a closed system....time plus chance"
Phrases coined and used in many places by the Christian apologetics of Francis Schaeffer.
Schaeffer, F.A. (1972). *He is there and he is not silent*. Wheaton: Tyndall House. (p. 54).

p.9

"I have seen the rise and fall of global dream worlds"
In other words I have seen the rise and fall of both global Communism and global Capitalism as utopian totalistic world-historical visions for the meaning of life and human flourishing. Global Communism is now a spent movement. Global Capitalism, on the other hand, gains momentum and dominance over the world but it is spiritually an empty shell. It is ideologically bankrupt where secularism, multiculturalism and political correctness both subvert and exclude higher or transcendent values.
Morse, S.B. (2002) *Dreamworld and catastrophe: the passing of mass utopia in East and West.* Cambridge: MIT Press.

"intellectual spears and long winged arrows of flaming thoughts"
Echoing the lines of William Blake "Our wars are wars of life, & wounds of love with intellectual spears & long winged arrows of thought." (Jerusalem 38:14)
Whitmarsh-Knight, D. (2009).*William Blake's Jerusalem explained*. Cambridge: William Blake Press. (p.212).

p.11

"the Owl of Minerva takes flight"
In ancient Greek mythology an Owl traditionally represented or accompanied Athena (the Roman Minerva) the virgin goddess of wisdom. Because of this association, the bird – often referred to as the "Owl of Athena" or the "Owl

of Minerva" — has been used as a symbol of knowledge, wisdom. The philosopher Hegel famously said: "the owl of Minerva spreads its wings only with the falling of the dusk"— meaning that philosophy comes to understand itself and its own period of history only after it has started to pass away. <https://en.wikipedia.org/wiki/Owl_of_Athena>

"Do not be deceived God is not mocked"

Bible, Galatians 6:7-8. "Do not be deceived: God cannot be mocked. A man reaps what he sows. The one who sows to please his sinful nature, from that nature will reap destruction; the one who sows to please the Spirit, from the Spirit will reap eternal life."

p.12

"The sun shall be turned into darkness, and the moon into blood."

Bible, Joel 2:31.

p.14

"the love which moves the sun and distant stars"

I echo here the closing lines of Dante's Divine Comedy (in Paradiso 33:145):

Dante (2008) *The divine comedy translated by Henry Wadsworth Longfellow with illustrations by Gustave Doré*. New York: Barnes & Noble. (p.693).

"that ancient heavenly connection to the starry dynamo"

This is a quote from Alan Ginsberg's HOWL.

Charters A (ed) (1992) *The portable beat reader*. London: Penguin Books. (p.62).

"Ariadne thread"

According to the Greek legend Theseus, the son of King Aegeus, volunteered to come and kill the Minotaur, which lived at the centre of a great labyrinth. Ariadne, who had fallen in love with Theseus, at first helped him by giving him a sword and a ball of thread, so that he could find his way out of the dark Minotaur's labyrinth once the deed was done.

<https://en.wikipedia.org/wiki/Ariadne>

p.15

"by good and necessary consequence"

The 'good and necessary consequence' clause of the Westminster Confession seeks to function as a bulwark of modern reformed protestant theology against modern cultural relativism and epistemological scepticism by mimicking deductive methods of empirical science and mathematics, but with long term disastrous results.

Bovell CR (2009) *By good and necessary consequence: a preliminary genealogy of biblicist foundationalism.* Oregon: WIPF & Stock.

p.19

"less than halfway through my tempestuous life"

I here echo the opening lines of Dante's Divine Comedy (Canto 1/1-3):

"Midway upon the journey of our life I found myself within a forest dark, for the straightforward pathway had been lost."

Dante (2008) *The divine comedy translated by Henry Wadsworth Longfellow with illustrations by Gustave Doré.* New York: Barnes & Noble. (p.693).

p.20

"Both inscape and landscape"

Inscape is a word coined by the poet Gerard Manley Hopkins. Hopkins thought "everything in the universe was characterised by what he called inscape, the distinctive design that constitutes individual identity.
<https://en.wikipedia.org/wiki/Inscape>

"mind-forged manacles"

Echoing here William Blake's poem *London:*

"In every cry of every Man,
In every Infants cry of fear,

In every voice: in every ban,
The mind-forg'd manacles I hear."

Stevenson, W. H. (1971). *Blake: the complete poems* (second edition). London: Longman. (p.155).

p.22

"counterfeit doubles of God"

Desmond, W (2008).*God and the between*. Malden: Blackwell Publishing. (p.61).

p.27

"Raziel"

Raziel (Hebrew: לאיזר 'Secrets of God'). Within Jewish legend and mysticism, the archangel Raziel is the chief 'Keeper of Secrets' and the 'Angel of Mysteries'.

See Louis Ginzberg's book, *The legends of the Jews, volume one: the book of Raziel* <http://philologos.org/__eb-lotj/vol1/two.htm#13>

p.28

"the doors of perception"

This echoes the title of the influential book by Aldous Huxley. But here the opening of the doors of perception is attributed, not to mescaline or some psychoactive drug, but to the work of the spirit opening all the five senses to the full spiritual reality of heaven earth and hell.

Huxley, A. (2004). *The doors of perception: and Heaven and Hell.* Vintage Classics.

p.30

"the valley of decision"

Bible: Joel 3:14

"Multitudes, multitudes
in the valley of decision!
For the day of the LORD
is near in the valley of decision."

p.33

"poemscapes"

Term coined by Kenneth Patchen.

Patchen, K (1970) *There's love all day: poems by Kenneth Patchen; selected by Dee Dabber* Barwick: Hallmark Editions. (p.53).

p.41

"the sun will shine for the children of wisdom at midnight"

Echoes the statement made by the 17th century Lutheran mystic Jacob Boehme: "There is a wonderful time coming. But because it begins in the night, there are many who shall not see it, because of their sleep and drunkenness; yet the sun will shine to the children at midnight."

Versluis, A. (1999). *Wisdom's children: A Christian esoteric tradition*. Albany: State University of New York Press. (p. 12).

p.42

"I saw the upper window of my soul filled with brilliance"

Echoes John Comenius' vision of Jesus appearing to him: "I pondered these things within myself and awaited what was to follow. Then behold, a bright light burst forth from above."

Comenius, J. (1997). *The labyrinth of the World and the paradise of the heart.* Paulest Press (Chapter 36). (Classics of Western Spirituality Series).

p.48

"when I see in the opening morn…'

Echoes Blake's *The Voice of the Ancient Bard:*

"Youth of delight! come hither and see the opening morn, image of truth new-born. Stevenson, W. H. (1971). *Blake The Complete Poems* (second edition). London: Longman. (p.73).

p.49

"angel-headed hipsters"

Echoing the first few lines of Alan Ginsberg's HOWL. Charters, A. (Ed.) (1992). *The portable beat reader*. Penguin Books. (p.68).

"on the nod over the body of bliss"

This line echoes the title of Alan Ginsberg's 1966 poem *Holy Ghost on the nod over the body of bliss* in Ginsberg, A. (2009). *Collected Poems 1947-1997.* Penguin Modern Classics.

p.50

"The Desolations of Moloch"

Moloch, also called Molech and Milcom, was a god of the Ancient Near East worshiped by the Ammonites (Bible, Acts 7:43), to whom children were sacrificed and 'made to pass through fire'.
See <https://en.wikipedia.org/wiki/Moloch>

Moloch appears in Allen Ginsberg's 1955 poem *Howl* as a great destroyer, corrupter, an alienator of human life under modern industrial conditions. To quote:

> "What sphinx of cement and aluminium bashed opened their skulls and ate up their brains and imaginations? Moloch! Solitude! Filth! Ugliness! Ashcans and unobtainable dollars! Children screaming under the stairways! Boys sobbing in armies! Old men weeping in the parks! Moloch! Moloch! Nightmare of Moloch! Moloch the loveless! Moloch! Moloch the heavy judger of men!"

Charters A. (Ed.) (1992). *The portable beat reader.* Penguin Books. (p.68).

As for Moloch's heavenly origin within the divine council and his catastrophic fall as an elohim or 'son of God' now stripped of his immortality and doomed to die, see:
Heiser, MS (2015). *The unseen realm: recovering the supernatural world of the Bible*: Hexham Press. (p.23-38). Also see Psalm 82.

p.52

"The Warrior of Light"

I have found wisdom, humour and inspiration from Paulo Coelho and his *Manual of the warrior of light.*
Coelho, P. (2003) *Manual of the warrior of light*. Harper Collins Publishing.

"a sword of lightening unsheathed consuming the scabbard"

A quotation from Shelly's A Defence of Poetry: "Poetry is a sword of lightening, ever unsheathed, which consumes the scabbard that would contain it."

Shelly, P.B. (2015) *A defence of poetry*. CreateSpace Independent Publishing Platform.

p.53

"feelings are just the visible face of invisible thinking"

Smart, J. (2015).*The little book of clarity: a quick guide to focus and declutter your mind*. Capstone. (p.47).

"....salvation through judgement"

Hamilton, James. (2010). *God's glory in salvation through judgement*. Wheaton: Crossway.

p.55

"Seeds of Light"

This a meditation on the words of Jesus as recorded in John 12:24-25 (the Bible):

"I assure you: Unless a grain of wheat falls to the ground and dies, it remains by itself. But if it dies, it produces a large crop. The one who loves his life will lose it, and the one who hates his life in this world will keep it for eternal life."

Seeds of Light also alludes to a story within Jewish Mysticism. "In the beginning, there was only God. But God decided to create the world by withdrawing his divine light and pouring it in to specially prepared vessels. Unfortunately, as God poured his light into the vessels, they shattered, sending sparks of God's divine light and shards of the vessels to every corner of creation. Our great task is to assist God by gathering the divine sparks back together and restoring the vessel to wholeness. Until all the sparks of God's light are gathered back together, the work of creation will not be complete. This task is called 'Tikun Olam' – the repair of the world."

As told within Michael Neill's Inside Out Revolution. Michael

(2013). *The inside out revolution: the only thing you need to know to change your life forever*. Hay House:London (p 117-118)

p.56

"Tree of Life"

Within the Christian tradition the Tree of Life can refer to the Church or to the Cross as the true Tree of Life or to the 'medicinal fruit of the Tree of Life which is Christ himself'. In Eastern Christianity the Tree of Life is the love of God. The original Tree of Eterna,l Life, according to the biblical narrative, stood at the centre of the Garden of Eden next to the Tree of the Knowledge of Good and Evil (Genesis 2:9). Other world religions use the term 'Tree of Life', giving it a wide variety of meanings, all of which signal theologically the original bliss, but also the narrative of a primordial Paradise lost and lamented, yearned for and pursued, within a temporal process, and a Paradise regained or found, either in this life or the next.

Milton J. (1990). *Paradise Lost* and *Paradise Regained.* Penguin. (Signet Classics). See also:

Comenius, J. (1997). *The labyrinth of the world and the paradise of the heart (Classics of Western Spirituality Series)*.Paulest Press.

In the biblical account a supratemporal Paradise 'lost' in time is protected from the encroachments of 'fallen time' by two cherubim with flaming swords flashing back and forth to guard the way to the Tree of Life (Genesis 3:24). Access to both the Tree of Life and to Paradise is granted through death to self and through 'new birth' in Christ crucified and raised from the dead as the 'first fruits' of the Tree of Life. See Luke 23:43. Also see:

<https://en.wikipedia.org/wiki/Tree_of_life>

p.58

"Selah"

Selah (/'si:l•/; Hebrew: סֶלָה), also transliterated as **sel•h**, occurs 74 times in the Hebrew bible, most frequently in the Psalms but also in Habakkuk. The origins and meaning of the word remain obscure. Various interpretations include

1) a musical notation 2) a pause for silence 3) a signal for worshippers to fall prostrate on the ground 4) a term for worshipers to cry out 5) a word meaning 'forever':
HCSB Study Bible (2009). Holman Bible Publishers. (p.2236). Also see https://en.wikipedia.org/wiki/Selah

"...how I do kiss and cherish your stones"

See The Bible: Revelation 21:19, Exodus 28:17. Some of the precious stones of the Heavenly Jerusalem also appear on the breastplate of Aaron the Israelite High Priest. Elsewhere they are associated with the Garden of Eden (Ezekiel 28:13). The gemstones at the foundation of the New Jerusalem are also historically associated with the 12 signs of the Zodiac.

Edwards Brothers Malloy
Thorofare, NJ USA
January 6, 2016